BRITISH SERIAL KILLERS COLOURING BOOK with Facts

Thank you for purchasing our "British Serial Killers Colouring Book with Facts".

The publication we have produced is not only an ordinary colouring book.
It serves as a factsheet. The material that lies in front of you constitutes part of the UK's dark history.
Not only the facials of serial killers are revealed, but in the background you will find places associated with them. You will discover their authentic items and their murder weapons.

This is a book made for those interested in serial killers. Here you will find a wealth of information.
You will learn dates and places of their birth and death. You will discover the nature of their crimes, number of victims and other real life facts of theirs.

For decades, the problem of serial killers has always arised numerous questions and evoked borderline emotions: from fear and horror to morbid fascination.

Our colouring book will shed more light onto the personalities of 30 serial killers from the UK that committed their crimes in the span of last 200 years. Some of them you've certainly heard of, some you're just about to meet. Feel invited to embark on a bloody and scary journey through the pages of this book of crimes.

No. 01/001

Stephen Akinmurele / The Cul-De-Sac Killer

FULL NAMES/OTHER NAMES

16 March 1978	Nigeria
DATE OF BIRTH	PLACE OF BIRTH
28 August 1999	21
DATE OF DEATH	AGED

DO NOT COPY

CRIMINAL HISTORY

NUMBER OF VICTIMS ☠ 5 – 7

METHOD OF MURDER ☚ strangulation

PENALTY/CAUSE OF DEATH ⚱ suicide by hanging

SPAN OF CRIMES 1995 – 1998

FINGERPRINT — No. 01 — No. 02

DATE   SIGNATURE

No. 01/002

Beverley Allitt / The Angel of Death

FULL NAMES/OTHER NAMES

4 October 1968	Grantham, Lincolnshire, England
DATE OF BIRTH	**PLACE OF BIRTH**
——	——
DATE OF DEATH	**AGED**

CRIMINAL HISTORY

NUMBER OF VICTIMS ☠ 4

METHOD OF MURDER — poisoning

PENALTY/CAUSE OF DEATH — 13 life sentences

SPAN OF CRIMES — February 1991 – April 1991

FINGERPRINT — No. 01   No. 02

DATE   **SIGNATURE**

No. 01/003

Levi Bellfield / The Hammer Man
FULL NAMES/OTHER NAMES

17 May 1968	Isleworth, London, England
DATE OF BIRTH	**PLACE OF BIRTH**
———	———
DATE OF DEATH	**AGED**

CRIMINAL HISTORY

NUMBER OF VICTIMS   ☠ 3 +

METHOD OF MURDER   🔨 hitting with a hammer

PENALTY/CAUSE OF DEATH   3 life sentences

SPAN OF CRIMES   21 March 2002 — 19 August 2004

FINGERPRINT   No. 01   No. 02

DATE   **SIGNATURE**

No. 01/004

Mary Ann Britland
FULL NAMES/OTHER NAMES

1847	Bolton, Lancashire, England
DATE OF BIRTH	PLACE OF BIRTH
9 August 1886	38 – 39
DATE OF DEATH	AGED

CRIMINAL HISTORY

NUMBER OF VICTIMS ☠ 3

METHOD OF MURDER poisoning

PENALTY/CAUSE OF DEATH hanged

SPAN OF CRIMES March 1886 – May 1886

FINGERPRINT   No. 01   No. 02

DATE   SIGNATURE

No. 01/005

Peter Bryan
FULL NAMES/OTHER NAMES

4 October 1969	London, England
DATE OF BIRTH	**PLACE OF BIRTH**

—	—
DATE OF DEATH	**AGED**

CRIMINAL HISTORY

NUMBER OF VICTIMS ☠ 3

METHOD OF MURDER
- hitting with a hammer
- strangulation

PENALTY/CAUSE OF DEATH hanged

SPAN OF CRIMES 1993 — 2004

FINGERPRINT No. 01 No. 02

DATE **SIGNATURE**

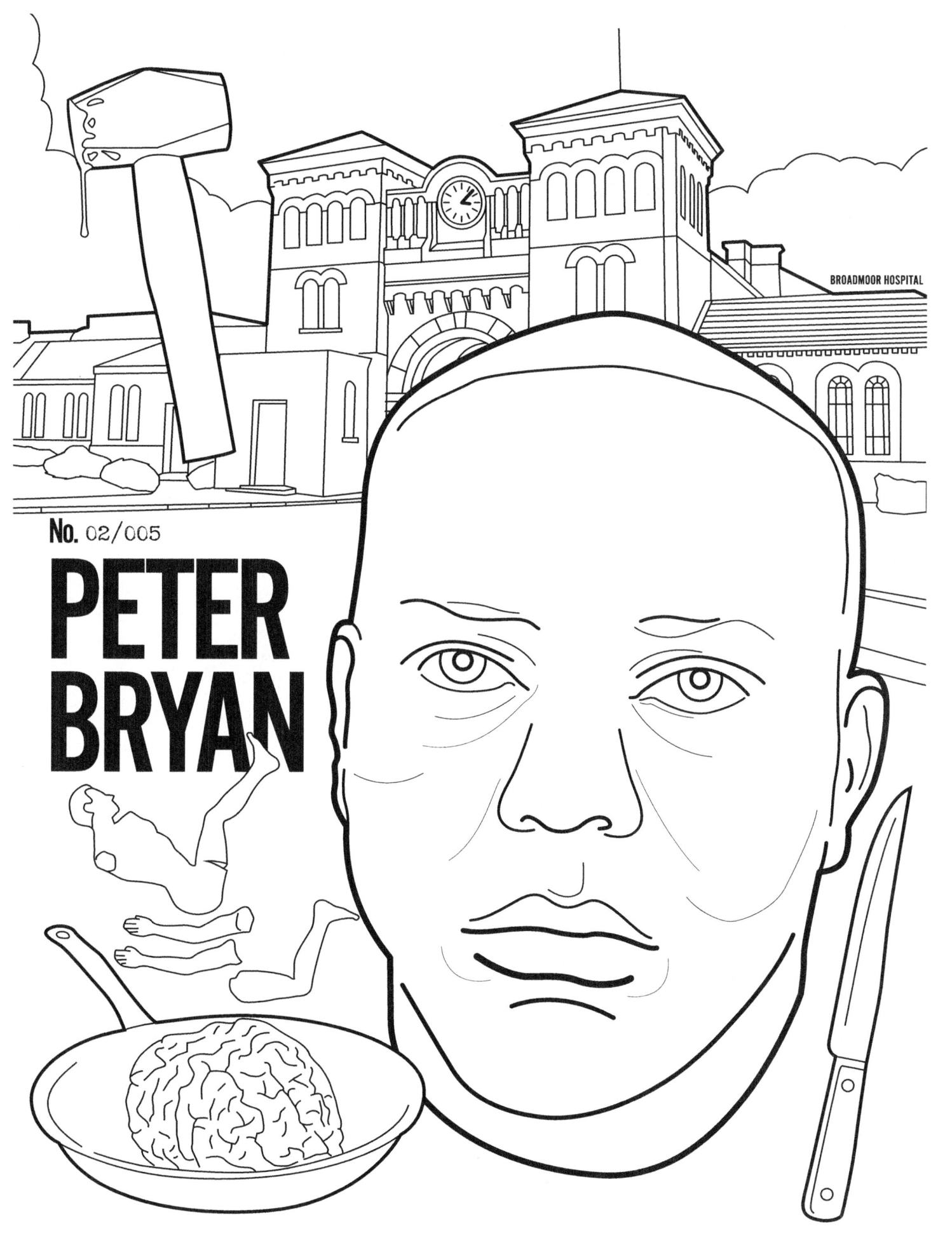

No. 01/006

George Chapman / Seweryn Kłosowski
FULL NAMES/OTHER NAMES

14 December 1865	Nagórna, Poland
DATE OF BIRTH	**PLACE OF BIRTH**
7 April 1903	37
DATE OF DEATH	**AGED**

CRIMINAL HISTORY

| **NUMBER OF VICTIMS** | ☠ 3 |

METHOD OF MURDER	☠ poisoning
PENALTY/CAUSE OF DEATH	⚰ hanged
SPAN OF CRIMES	1897 — 1902

FINGERPRINT   No. 01   No. 02

DATE   **SIGNATURE**

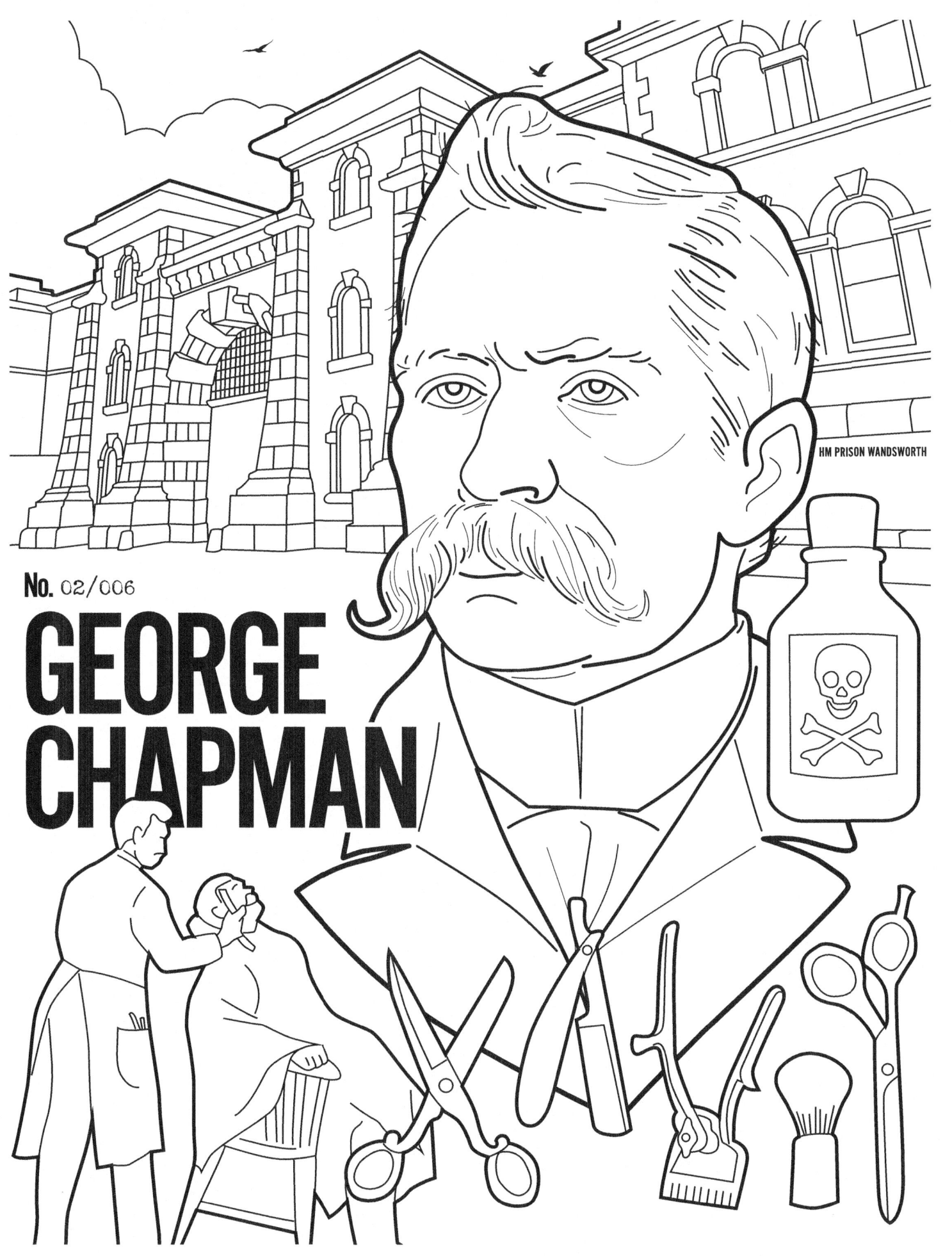

№ 01/007

John Childs / Bruce Childs

FULL NAMES/OTHER NAMES

unknown
DATE OF BIRTH

unknown
PLACE OF BIRTH

—
DATE OF DEATH

—
AGED

CRIMINAL HISTORY

NUMBER OF VICTIMS ☠ 6

- strangulation
- stabbing with knife and sword
- shooting

METHOD OF MURDER

life imprisonment
PENALTY/CAUSE OF DEATH

1974 — 1978
SPAN OF CRIMES

FINGERPRINT   No. 01   No. 02

DATE   **SIGNATURE**

No. 01/008

Robert George Clements / Dr Bluebeard

FULL NAMES/OTHER NAMES

1880	Belfast, Ireland
DATE OF BIRTH	PLACE OF BIRTH
1947	67
DATE OF DEATH	AGED

CRIMINAL HISTORY

NUMBER OF VICTIMS	1 – 4

METHOD OF MURDER	poisoning
PENALTY/CAUSE OF DEATH	suicide
SPAN OF CRIMES	1920 – 1947

FINGERPRINT — No. 01 — No. 02

DATE   SIGNATURE

No. 01/009

Mary Ann Cotton / Mary Ann Robson
FULL NAMES/OTHER NAMES

31 October 1832	Low Moorsley, England
DATE OF BIRTH	**PLACE OF BIRTH**
24 March 1873	40
DATE OF DEATH	**AGED**

CRIMINAL HISTORY

NUMBER OF VICTIMS ☠ 21 +

METHOD OF MURDER	🍾 poisoning
PENALTY/CAUSE OF DEATH	⚮ hanged
SPAN OF CRIMES	1857 – 1872

DO NOT COPY

FINGERPRINT

No. 01   No. 02

DATE   **SIGNATURE**

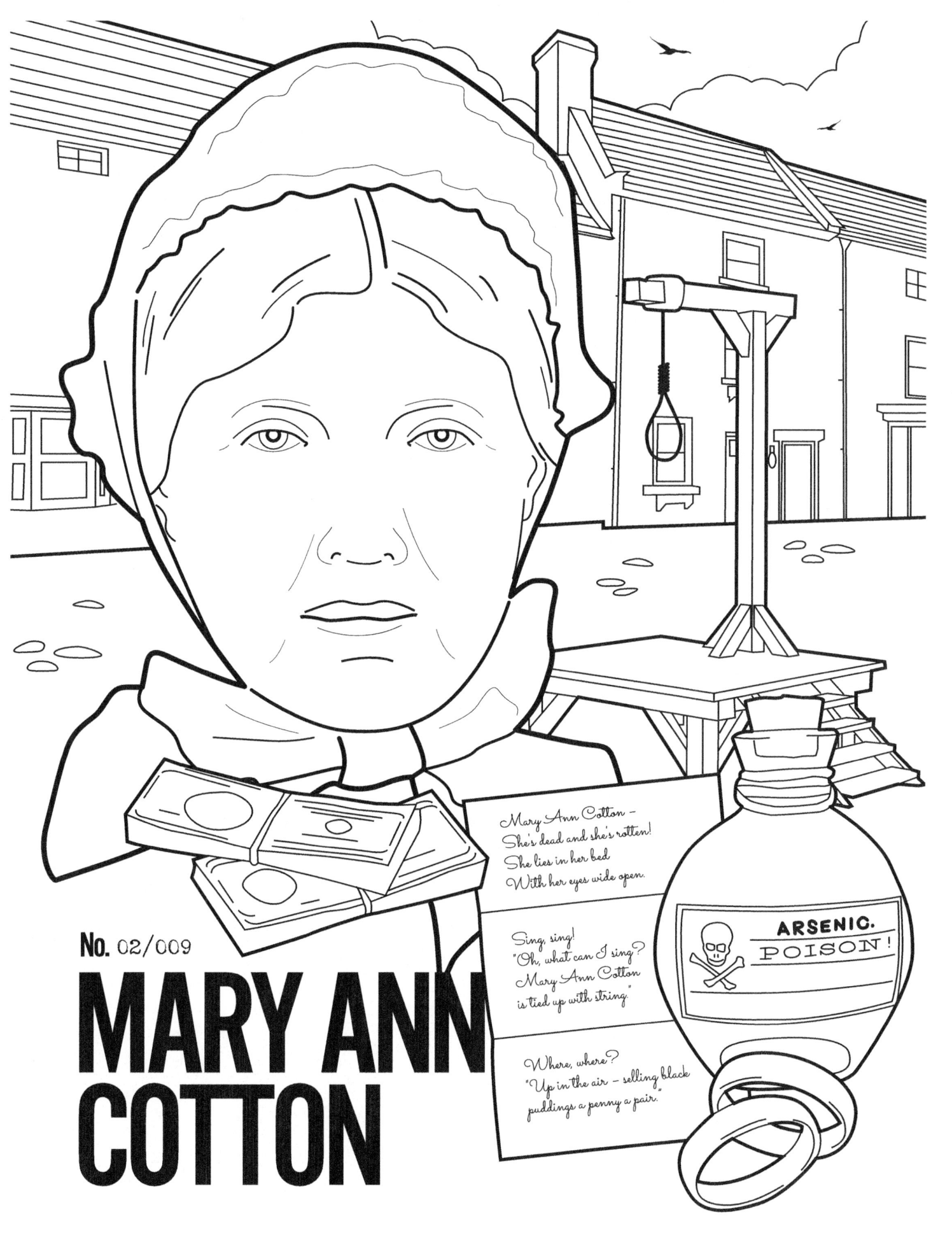

No. 01/010

Gordon Cummins / The Blackout Ripper

FULL NAMES/OTHER NAMES

18 February 1914	New Earswick, North Yorkshire, England
DATE OF BIRTH	PLACE OF BIRTH
25 June 1942	28
DATE OF DEATH	AGED

CRIMINAL HISTORY

NUMBER OF VICTIMS ☠ 4—6

METHOD OF MURDER
- strangulation
- stabbing with knife

PENALTY/CAUSE OF DEATH
- hanged

SPAN OF CRIMES: 1941 — 1942

| FINGERPRINT | No. 01 | No. 02 |

DATE   SIGNATURE

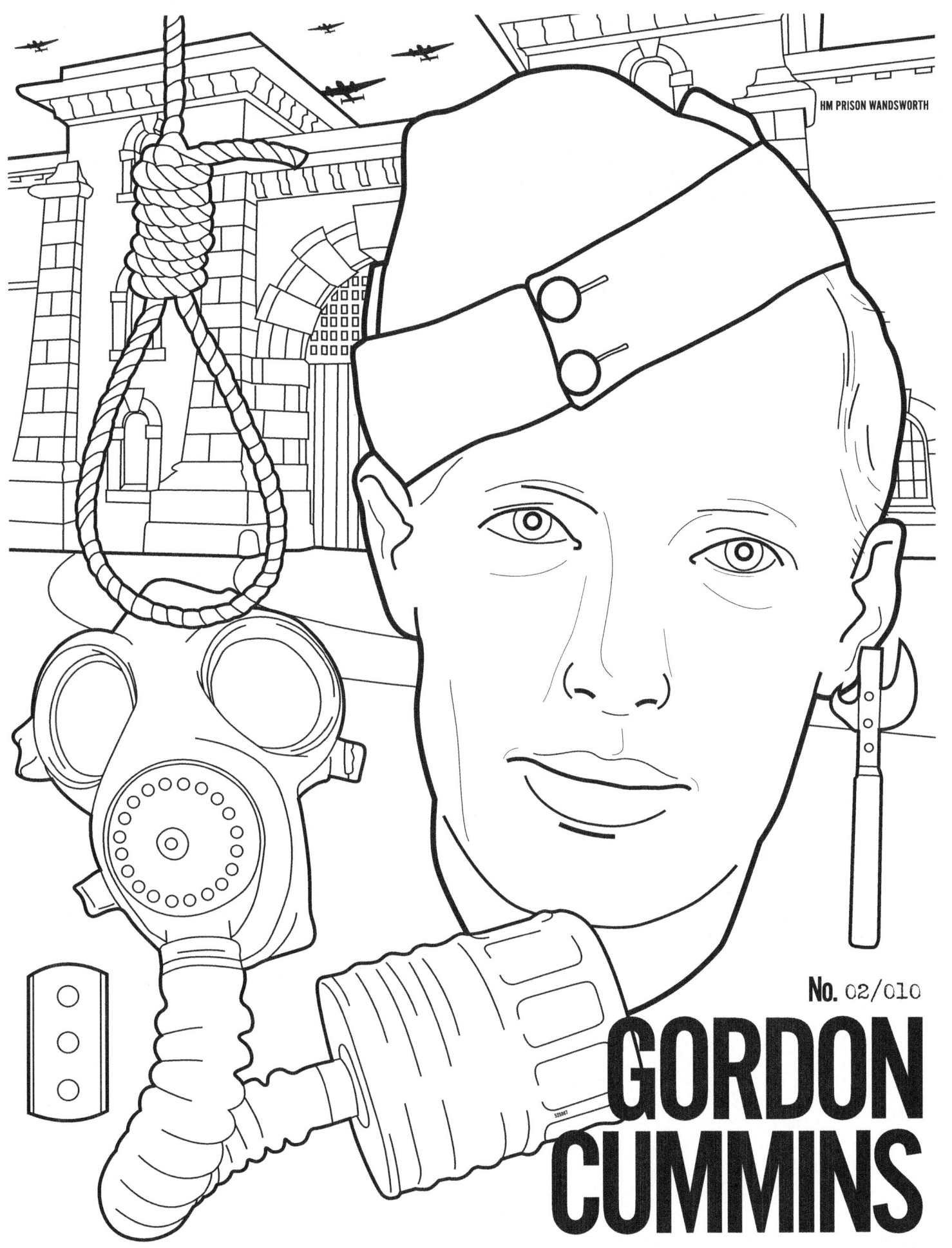

No. 01/011

Frederick Bailey Deeming / The Windsor Murderer
FULL NAMES/OTHER NAMES

30 July 1853	Ashby-de-la-Zouch, Leicestershire, England
DATE OF BIRTH	PLACE OF BIRTH
23 May 1892	38
DATE OF DEATH	AGED

CRIMINAL HISTORY

NUMBER OF VICTIMS ☠ 6

METHOD OF MURDER	🪓 beating with an axe
PENALTY/CAUSE OF DEATH	⚰ hanged
SPAN OF CRIMES	1891 – 1892

FINGERPRINT — No. 01 — No. 02

DATE SIGNATURE

No. 01/012

Amelia Dyer / The Reading Baby Farmer

FULL NAMES/OTHER NAMES

1836	Pyle Marsh, Bristol, England
DATE OF BIRTH	PLACE OF BIRTH
10 June 1896	59/60
DATE OF DEATH	AGED

CRIMINAL HISTORY

NUMBER OF VICTIMS ☠ 6 – 100 +

METHOD OF MURDER ☞ strangulation

PENALTY/CAUSE OF DEATH ⚰ hanged

SPAN OF CRIMES 1880 – 1896

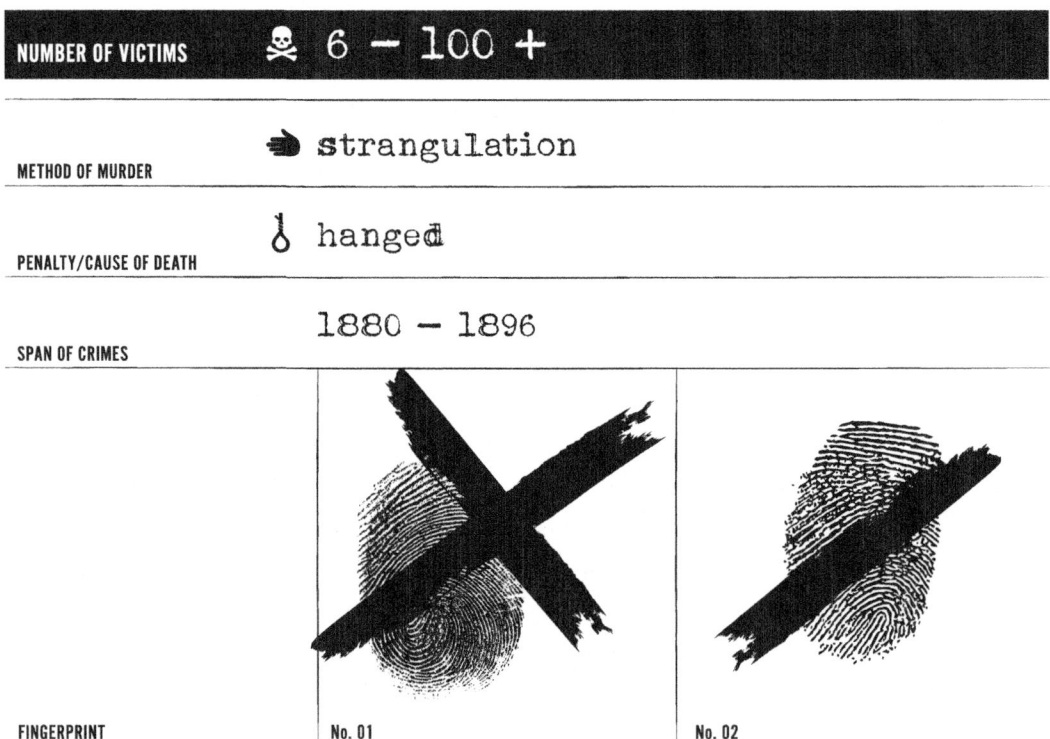

FINGERPRINT   No. 01   No. 02

DATE   SIGNATURE

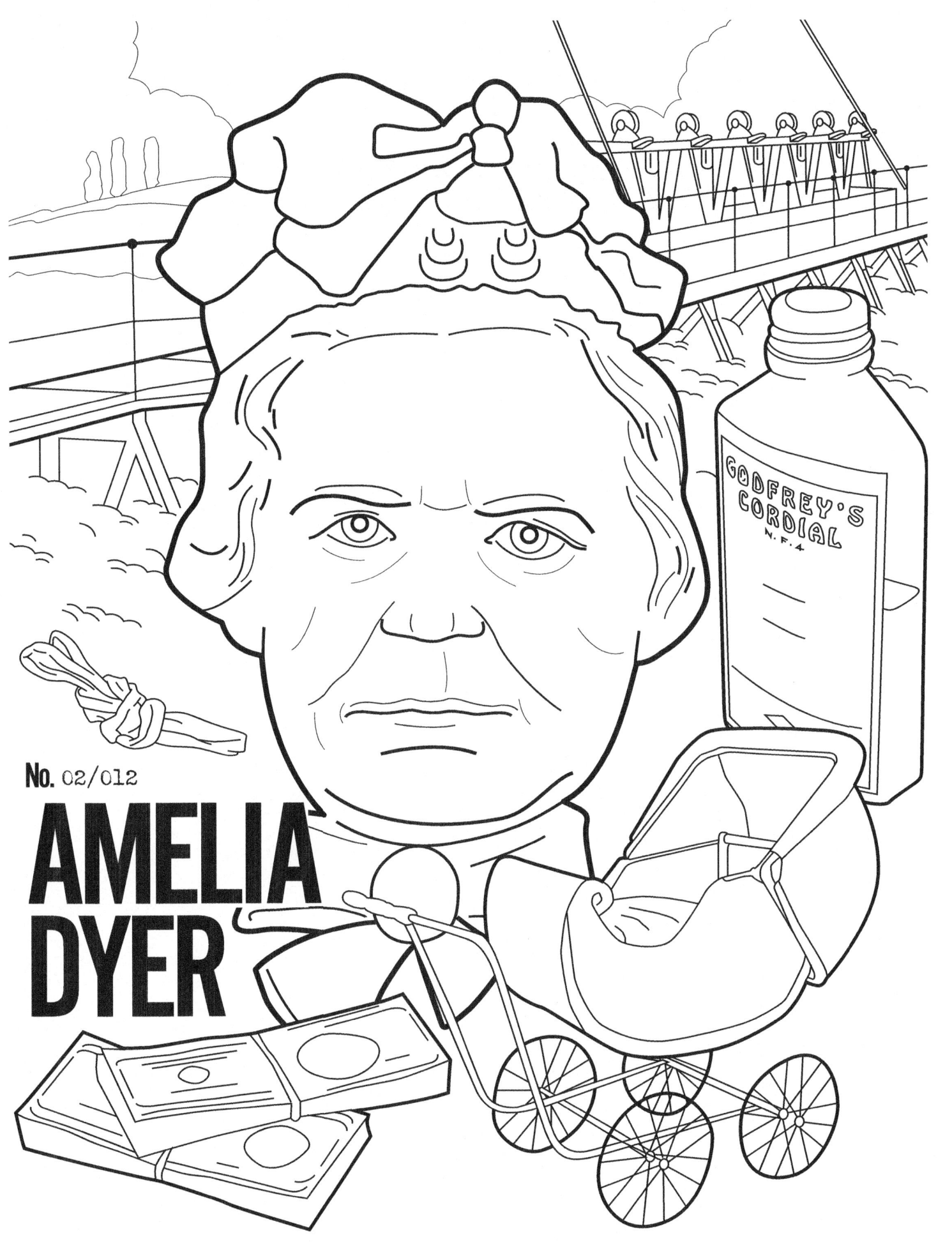

No. 01/013

John Haigh / The Acid Bath Murderer

FULL NAMES/OTHER NAMES

24 July 1909	Stamford, Lincolnshire, England
DATE OF BIRTH	PLACE OF BIRTH
10 August 1949	40
DATE OF DEATH	AGED

CRIMINAL HISTORY

NUMBER OF VICTIMS ☠ 6 — 9

METHOD OF MURDER
- beating with a blunt instrument
- shooting

PENALTY/CAUSE OF DEATH
- hanged

SPAN OF CRIMES 1944 — 1949

FINGERPRINT No. 01 No. 02

DATE SIGNATURE

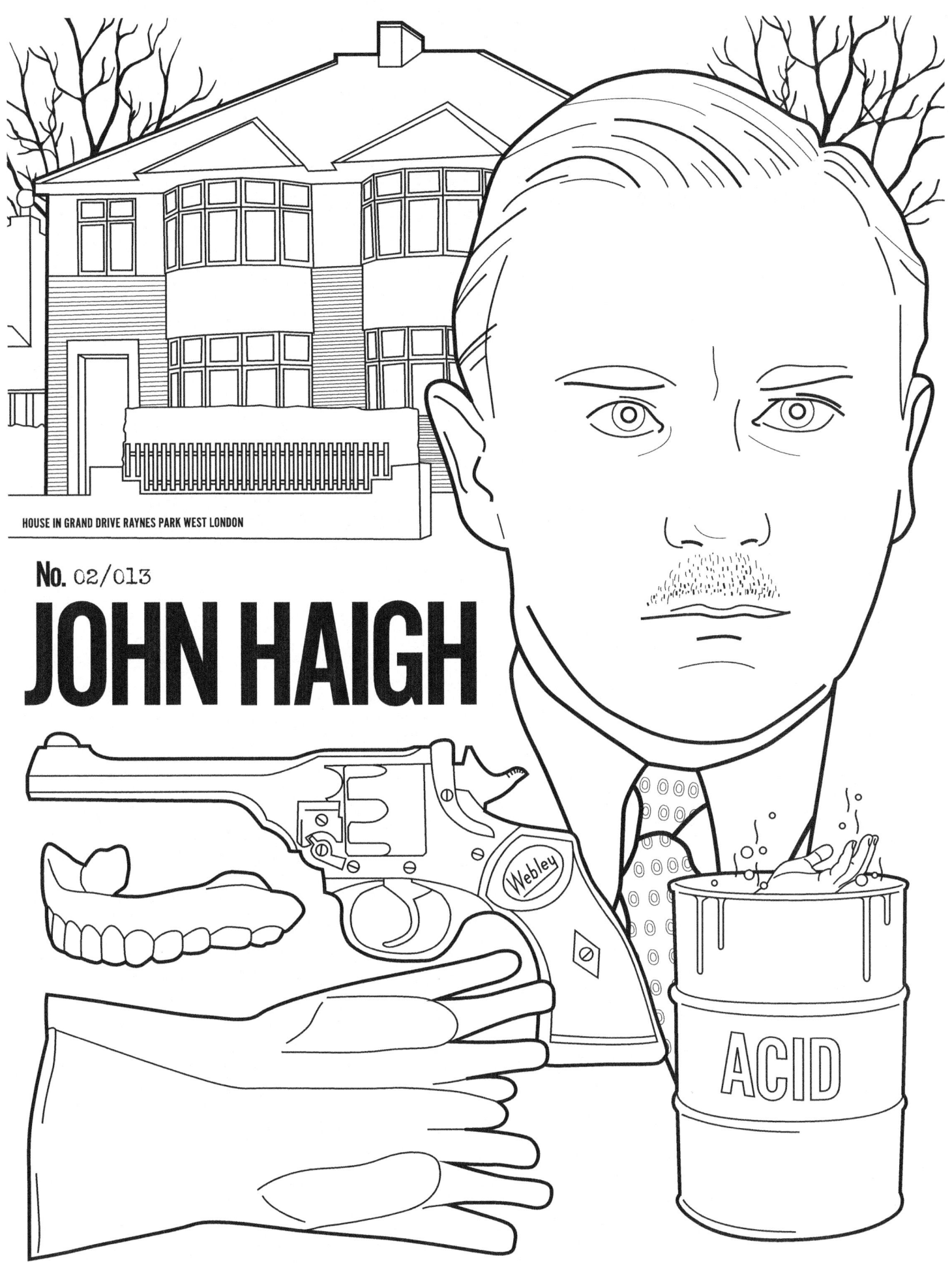

No. 01/014

Anthony Hardy / The Camden Ripper

FULL NAMES/OTHER NAMES

31 May 1951	Burton upon Trent, Staffordshire, England
DATE OF BIRTH	PLACE OF BIRTH
26 November 2020	69
DATE OF DEATH	AGED

CRIMINAL HISTORY

NUMBER OF VICTIMS ☠ 3 – 9 +

METHOD OF MURDER ✋ strangulation

PENALTY/CAUSE OF DEATH life imprisonment

SPAN OF CRIMES 2002

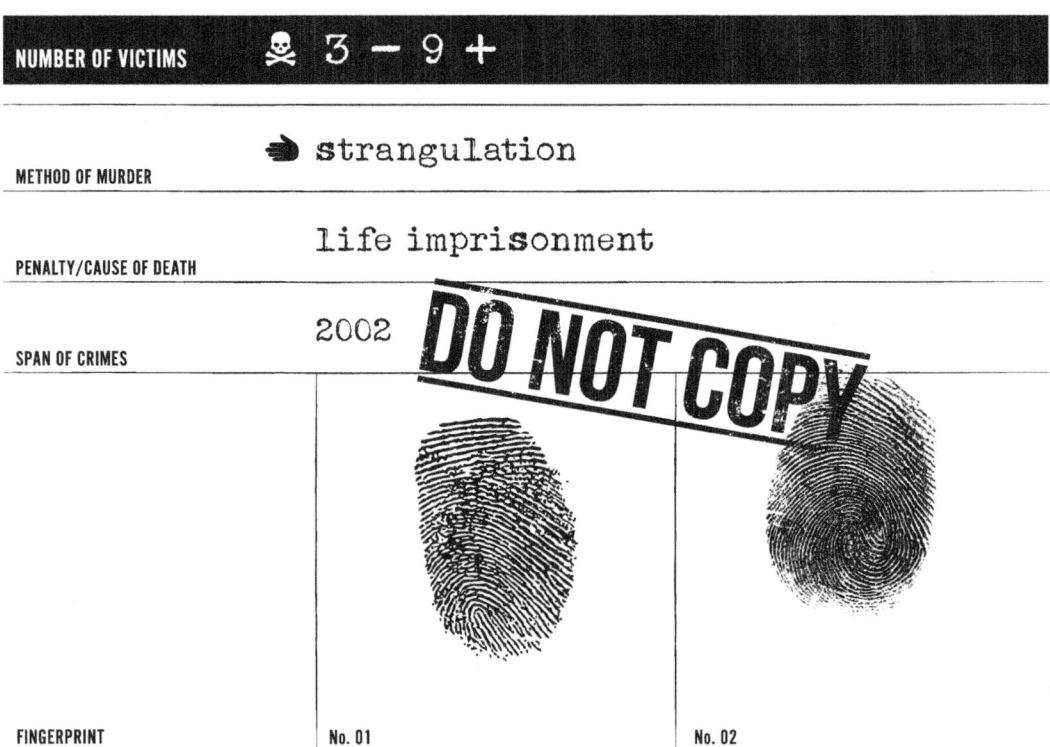

FINGERPRINT — No. 01 — No. 02

DATE   SIGNATURE

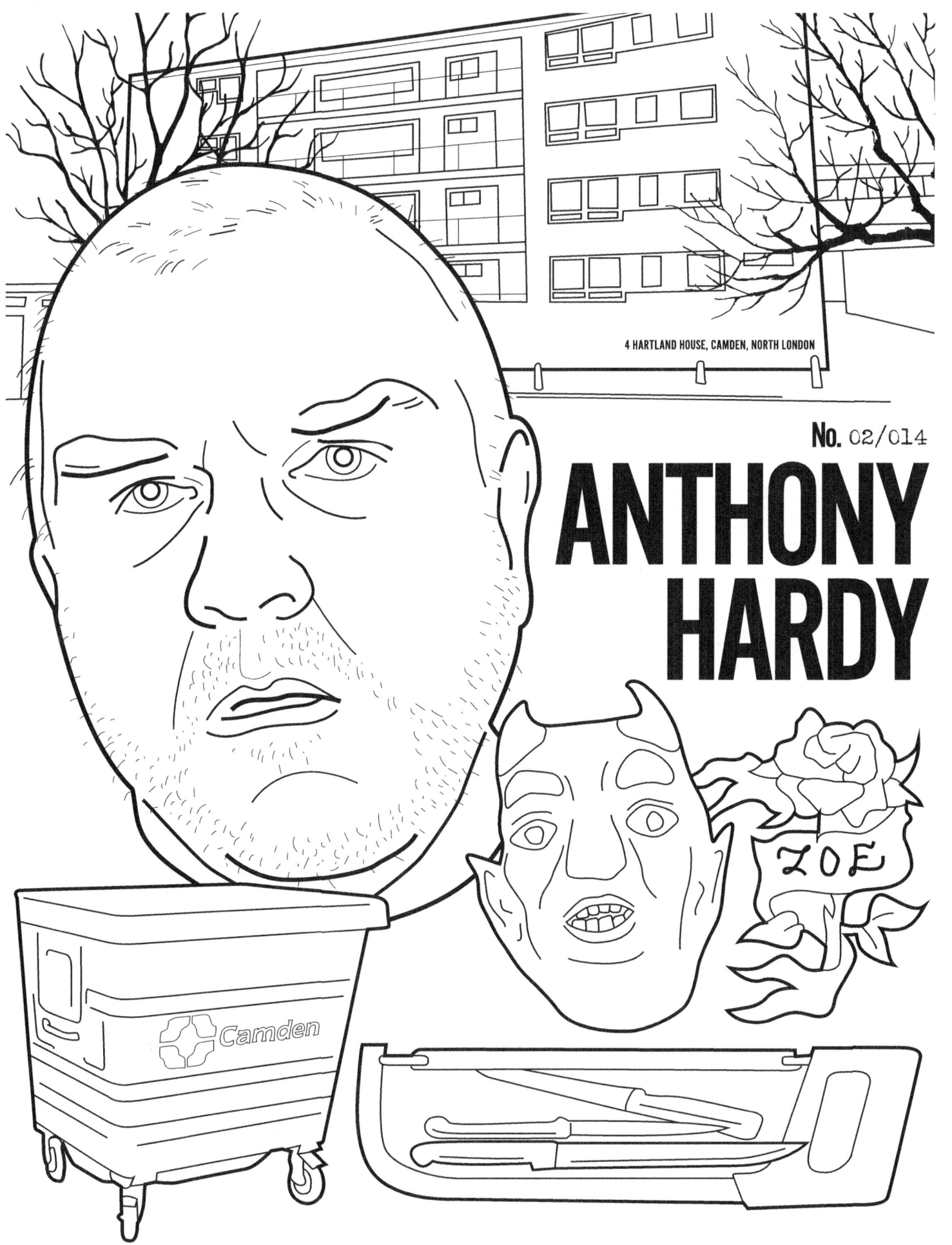

No. 01/015

Patrick Mackay / The Psychopath

FULL NAMES/OTHER NAMES

25 September 1952

DATE OF BIRTH

Dartford, Kent, England

PLACE OF BIRTH

—

DATE OF DEATH

AGED

DO NOT COPY

CRIMINAL HISTORY

NUMBER OF VICTIMS ☠ 3 – 11

METHOD OF MURDER / stabbing with knife

PENALTY/CAUSE OF DEATH life imprisonment

SPAN OF CRIMES February 1974 – March 1975

DATE   SIGNATURE

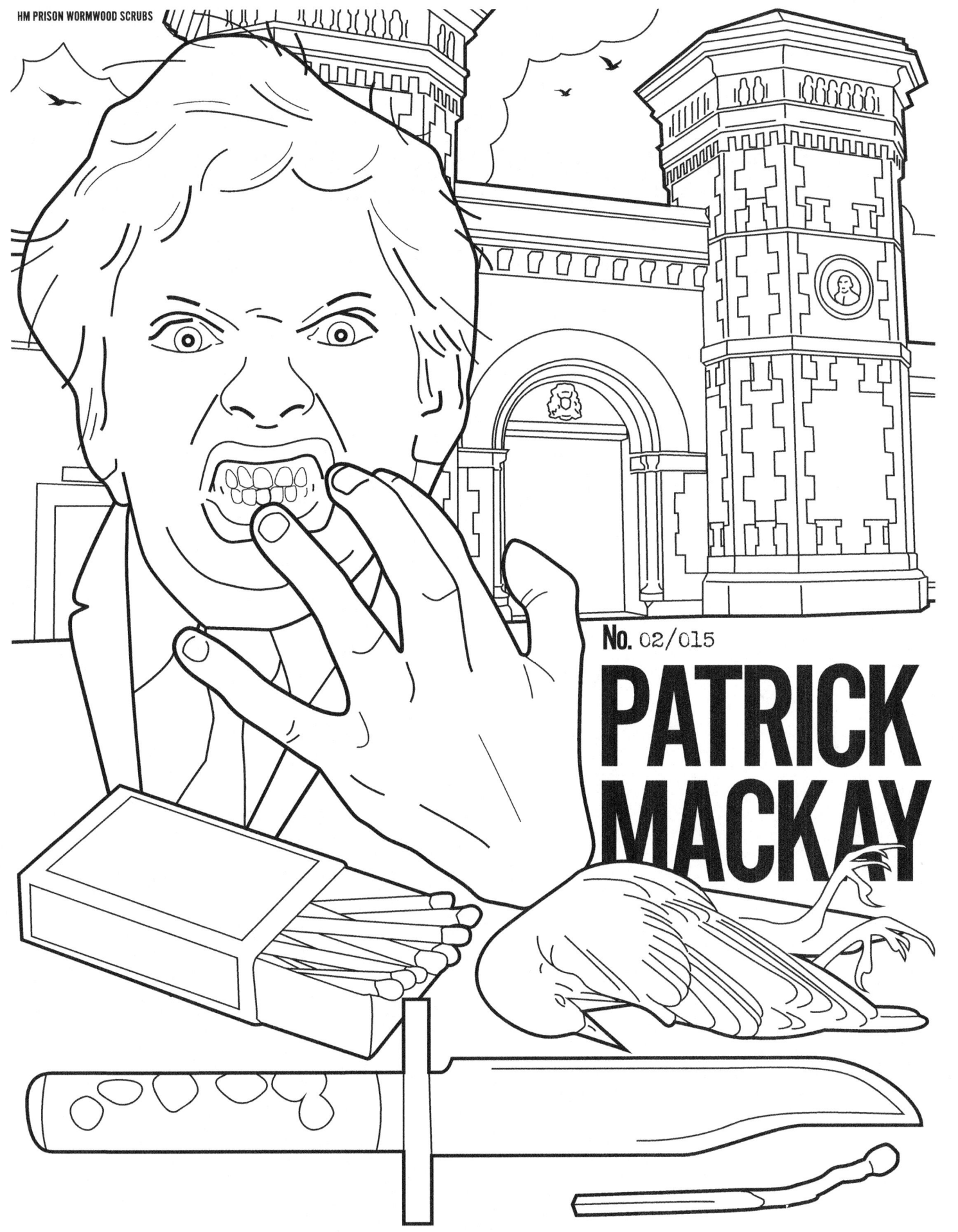

No. 01/016

Donald Neilson / The Black Panther
FULL NAMES/OTHER NAMES

1 August 1936	Bradford, England
DATE OF BIRTH	PLACE OF BIRTH
18 December 2011	75
DATE OF DEATH	AGED

CRIMINAL HISTORY

NUMBER OF VICTIMS ☠ 1 – 3

METHOD OF MURDER shooting

PENALTY/CAUSE OF DEATH life imprisonment

SPAN OF CRIMES 1974 – 1975

DO NOT COPY

FINGERPRINT — No. 01 — No. 02

DATE — SIGNATURE

No. 01/017

Dennis Nilsen / The Muswell Hill Murderer

FULL NAMES/OTHER NAMES

23 November 1945	Fraserburgh, Aberdeenshire, Scotland
DATE OF BIRTH	PLACE OF BIRTH
12 May 2018	72
DATE OF DEATH	AGED

CRIMINAL HISTORY

NUMBER OF VICTIMS ☠ 12 – 15

METHOD OF MURDER: ligature strangulation

PENALTY/CAUSE OF DEATH: life imprisonment

SPAN OF CRIMES: 30 December 1978 – 26 January 1983

FINGERPRINT   No. 01   No. 02

DATE   SIGNATURE

No. 01/018

Harold Shipman / Doctor Death
FULL NAMES/OTHER NAMES

14 January 1946	Nottingham, Nottinghamshire, England
DATE OF BIRTH	PLACE OF BIRTH
13 January 2004	57
DATE OF DEATH	AGED

CRIMINAL HISTORY

NUMBER OF VICTIMS ☠ 215 +

METHOD OF MURDER	🧪 poisoning
PENALTY/CAUSE OF DEATH	🪢 suicide by hanging
SPAN OF CRIMES	1975 – 1998

FINGERPRINT — No. 01 — No. 02

DATE   SIGNATURE

No. 01/019

Peter Sutcliffe / The Yorkshire Ripper
FULL NAMES/OTHER NAMES

2 June 1946	Bingley, West Riding of Yorkshire, England
DATE OF BIRTH	**PLACE OF BIRTH**
13 November 2020	74
DATE OF DEATH	**AGED**

CRIMINAL HISTORY

NUMBER OF VICTIMS ☠ 1 – 12

METHOD OF MURDER	↗ hitting with a hammer ／ stabbing with knife
PENALTY/CAUSE OF DEATH	life imprisonment
SPAN OF CRIMES	1975 – 1980

DATE   SIGNATURE

No. 01/020

George Joseph Smith / The Brides in the Bath Murders
FULL NAMES/OTHER NAMES

11 January 1872	Bethnal Green, London, England
DATE OF BIRTH	PLACE OF BIRTH
13 August 1915	43
DATE OF DEATH	AGED

CRIMINAL HISTORY

NUMBER OF VICTIMS ☠ 3

METHOD OF MURDER ≋ drowning

PENALTY/CAUSE OF DEATH ⚲ hanged

SPAN OF CRIMES 1912 – 1914

FINGERPRINT — No. 01 — No. 02

DATE   SIGNATURE

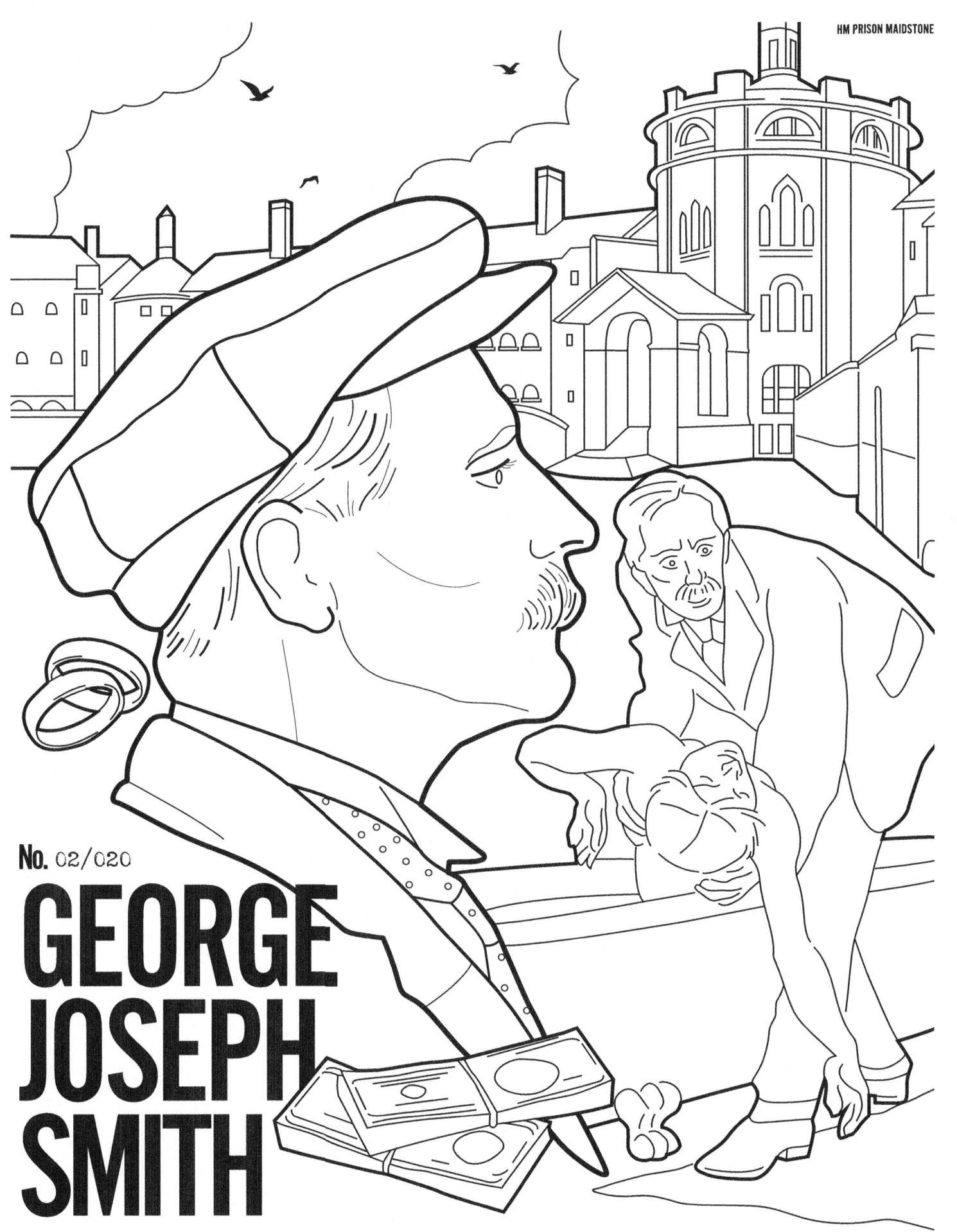

No. 01/021

John Straffen
FULL NAMES/OTHER NAMES

27 February 1930	Bordon Camp, Hampshire, England
DATE OF BIRTH	PLACE OF BIRTH
19 November 2007	77
DATE OF DEATH	AGED

CRIMINAL HISTORY

NUMBER OF VICTIMS ☠ 3

METHOD OF MURDER strangulation

PENALTY/CAUSE OF DEATH death (commuted to life imprisonment)

SPAN OF CRIMES 15 July 1951 – 29 April 1952

FINGERPRINT   No. 01   No. 02

DATE   SIGNATURE

No. 01/022

Mary Elizabeth Wilson / The Merry Widow of Windy Nook
FULL NAMES/OTHER NAMES

1889	Catchgate, Stanley, Durham, England
DATE OF BIRTH	PLACE OF BIRTH
1963	73—74
DATE OF DEATH	AGED

CRIMINAL HISTORY

NUMBER OF VICTIMS   ☠ 2 — 4

METHOD OF MURDER   🍶 poisoning

PENALTY/CAUSE OF DEATH   death (commuted to life imprisonment)

SPAN OF CRIMES   1955 — 1957

FINGERPRINT   No. 01   No. 02

DATE   SIGNATURE

No. 01/023

Graham Young / The Teacup Poisoner
FULL NAMES/OTHER NAMES

7 September 1947	Neasden, Middlesex, England
DATE OF BIRTH	PLACE OF BIRTH
1 August 1990	42
DATE OF DEATH	AGED

CRIMINAL HISTORY

NUMBER OF VICTIMS ☠ 3 +

METHOD OF MURDER	poisoning
PENALTY/CAUSE OF DEATH	life imprisonment / heart attack
SPAN OF CRIMES	1962 — 1971

FINGERPRINT — No. 01 — No. 02

DATE   SIGNATURE

No. 01/024

Robert Black / Smelly Bob
FULL NAMES/OTHER NAMES

21 April 1947	Grangemouth, Scotland
DATE OF BIRTH	**PLACE OF BIRTH**
12 January 2016	68
DATE OF DEATH	**AGED**

DO NOT COPY

CRIMINAL HISTORY

NUMBER OF VICTIMS   ☠ 4 +

METHOD OF MURDER   strangulation

PENALTY/CAUSE OF DEATH   life imprisonment / heart attack

SPAN OF CRIMES   1981 – 1986

FINGERPRINT   No. 01   No. 02

DATE   **SIGNATURE**

No. 01/025

Archibald Hall / Roy Fontaine
FULL NAMES/OTHER NAMES

17 June 1924	Glasgow, Scotland
DATE OF BIRTH	PLACE OF BIRTH
16 September 2002	78
DATE OF DEATH	AGED

CRIMINAL HISTORY

NUMBER OF VICTIMS ☠ 5

METHOD OF MURDER
- shooting
- suffocation
- beating with a spade
- beating with a poker

PENALTY/CAUSE OF DEATH
life imprisonment

SPAN OF CRIMES
1977 – 1978

FINGERPRINT   No. 01   No. 02

DATE   SIGNATURE

No. 01/026

Peter Manuel / The Beast of Birkenshaw
FULL NAMES/OTHER NAMES

13 March 1927	New York City, US
DATE OF BIRTH	PLACE OF BIRTH
11 July 1958	31
DATE OF DEATH	AGED

CRIMINAL HISTORY

NUMBER OF VICTIMS	☠ 7 +
METHOD OF MURDER	shooting
PENALTY/CAUSE OF DEATH	hanged
SPAN OF CRIMES	1956 – 1958

DATE   SIGNATURE

No. 01/027

Edward William Pritchard
FULL NAMES/OTHER NAMES

6 December 1825	Southsea, Hampshire, England
DATE OF BIRTH	PLACE OF BIRTH
28 July 1865	40
DATE OF DEATH	AGED

CRIMINAL HISTORY

NUMBER OF VICTIMS ☠ 2+

METHOD OF MURDER — poisoning

PENALTY/CAUSE OF DEATH — hanged

SPAN OF CRIMES — February 28 – March 18, 1865

FINGERPRINT No. 01 No. 02

DATE SIGNATURE

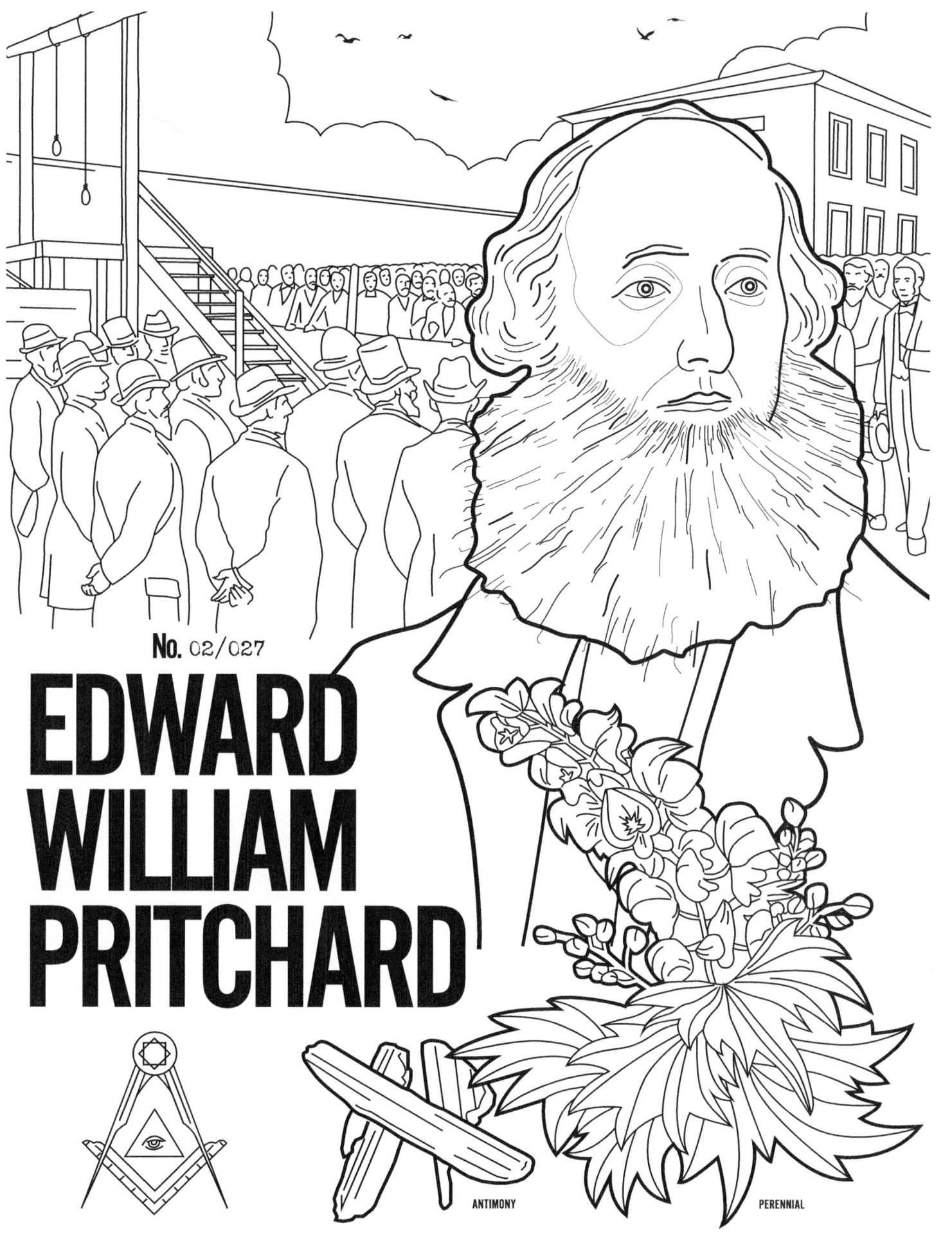

No. 01/028

Peter Tobin

FULL NAMES/OTHER NAMES

27 August 1946	Johnstone, Renfrewshire, Scotland
DATE OF BIRTH	PLACE OF BIRTH
—	—
DATE OF DEATH	AGED

CRIMINAL HISTORY

NUMBER OF VICTIMS ☠ 3+

METHOD OF MURDER	✓ stabbing with knife
PENALTY/CAUSE OF DEATH	life imprisonment
SPAN OF CRIMES	February 10 / August 5, 1991 September 24, 2006

FINGERPRINT	No. 01	No. 02

DATE SIGNATURE

No. 01/029

John Cooper / The Bullseye Killer

FULL NAMES/OTHER NAMES

3 September 1944	Milford Haven, Pembrokeshire, Wales
DATE OF BIRTH	**PLACE OF BIRTH**
—	—
DATE OF DEATH	**AGED**

CRIMINAL HISTORY

NUMBER OF VICTIMS ☠ 4

METHOD OF MURDER shooting

PENALTY/CAUSE OF DEATH life imprisonment

SPAN OF CRIMES 1985 – 1989

FINGERPRINT   No. 01   No. 02

DO NOT COPY

DATE   **SIGNATURE**

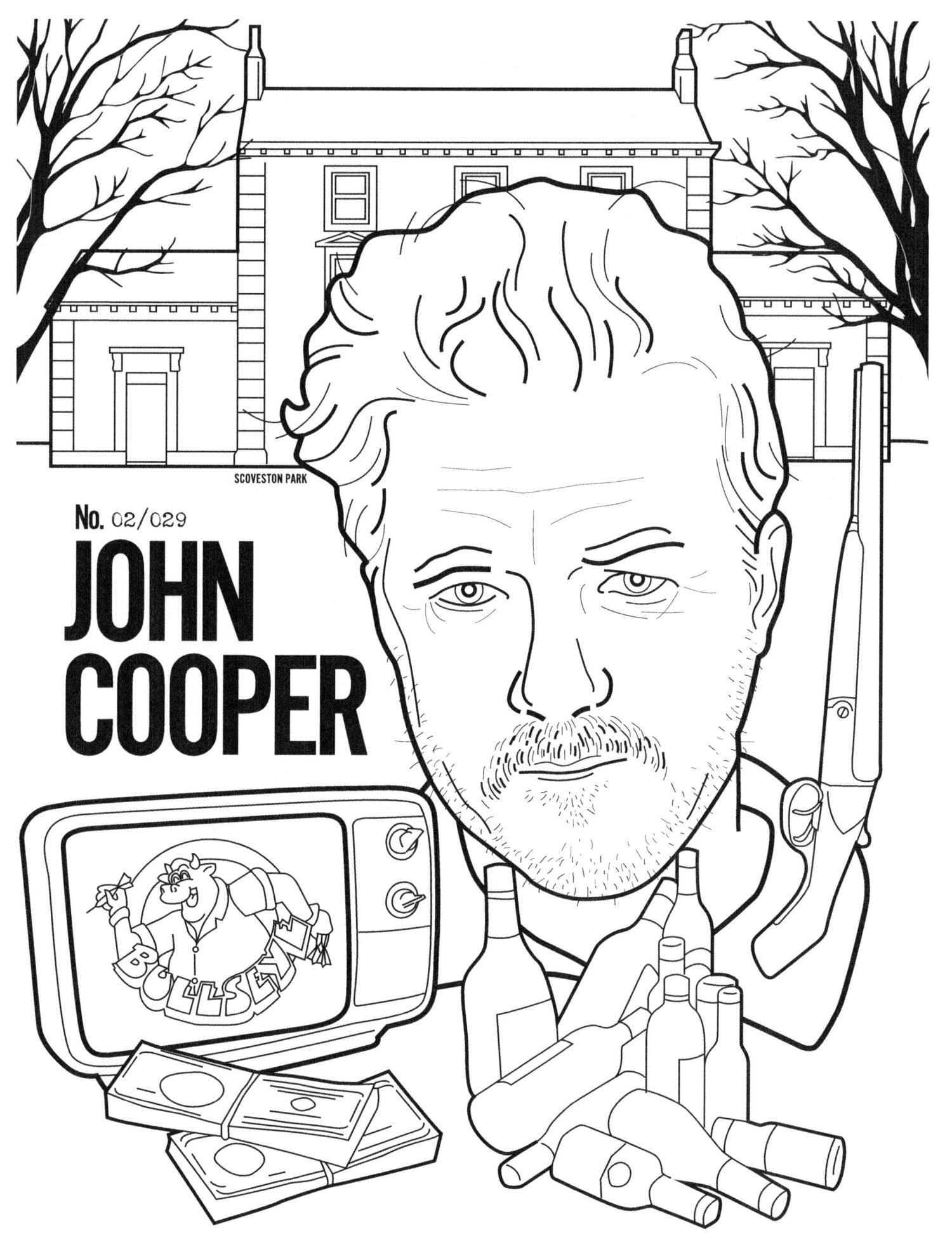

No. 01/030

Peter Moore / The Man In Black

FULL NAMES/OTHER NAMES

19 September 1946	St Helens, Lancashire, England
DATE OF BIRTH	PLACE OF BIRTH
——	——
DATE OF DEATH	AGED

CRIMINAL HISTORY

NUMBER OF VICTIMS ☠ 4

METHOD OF MURDER: stabbing with knife

PENALTY/CAUSE OF DEATH: life imprisonment

SPAN OF CRIMES: September – December 1995

FINGERPRINT No. 01 No. 02

DATE SIGNATURE

THIS BOOK BELONGS TO:

No. 00/000

FULL NAMES/OTHER NAMES
_____

DATE OF BIRTH
_____

PLACE OF BIRTH

ADDRESS
_____

AGED

DATE   SIGNATURE
_____

DO NOT COPY

IT'S JUST A GRAPHIC DESIGN IDEA.

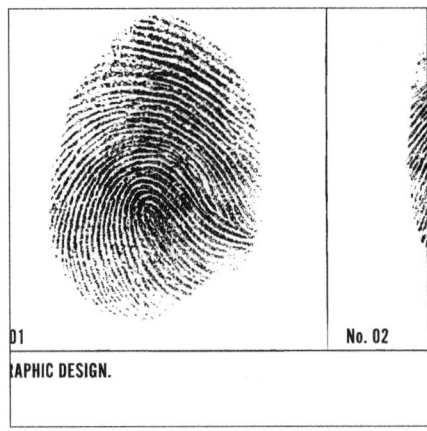

01   No. 02
:APHIC DESIGN.

The fingerprints shown in this book are not real.

All rights reserved. No part of these publications may be reproduced, distributed, or transmitted in any form or by any means, including photocopying, recording, or other electronic or mechanical methods, without the prior written permission of the publisher, except in the case of brief quotations embodied in critical reviews and certain other noncommercial uses permitted by copyright law.

Printed in Great Britain
by Amazon